Predicaments

Predicaments

Francis B. Nyamnjoh

Langaa Research & Publishing CIG
Mankon, Bamenda

Publisher:
Langaa RPCIG
Langaa Research & Publishing Common Initiative Group
P.O. Box 902 Mankon
Bamenda
North West Region
Cameroon
Langaagrp@gmail.com
www.langaa-rpcig.net

Distributed outside N. America by African Books
Collective
orders@africanbookscollective.com
www.africanbookscollective.com

Distributed in N. America by Michigan State
University Press
msupress@msu.edu
www.msupress.msu.edu

ISBN: 9956-579-27-0

DISCLAIMER

Contents

6. Outrage and Hope

7. Ignorance and Freedom

8. Power and Resistance

9. Peacemakers

10. Certain and Uncertain

Foreword

Francis Nyamnjoh is a playwright and much more, but he is best known for his novels, so seeing his name associated with poetry is somewhat surprising. However, for those familiar with Nyamnjoh's writing, the initial awkwardness dissipates as the sociological insights of his poems begin to emerge. Interestingly, Nyamnjoh points out that this publication is decades "late" in that the poems were written in his college and undergraduate years in Cameroon. Accordingly, with this collection of juvenilia, Nyamnjoh takes the reader back in time, even as the past catches up with the present, to show how unchanging and even painful life can be.

In a volume with ten sections, Nyamnjoh comments on society by addressing a wide range of issues, from unacceptable privileges, through disturbing cruelty, and flawed leadership to the certainties and uncertainties of love and life as a whole, indicating that the seeds of this scholar's attraction to sociological concerns were planted at a young age. As a result, by using poetry this time, and effectively too, one is left wondering if Nyamnjoh has not simply returned to a starting point he abandoned decades ago to rush his ideas to the public in an otherwise more accessible genre—the novel.

Thematically and stylistically, the bulk of Nyamnjoh's poems are direct and easy to understand, yet there are some that are abstract and obscure. Consequently, there are poems in this volume that one will remember and others that will leave one indifferent—as the potential elusiveness of some of the poems, a quality reminiscent of modernist poetry, could be somewhat frustrating. This notwithstanding, the economy in structure, even within a single poem, all too often yields a thematic breadth that leaves the reader baffled, just like the poet who seems himself at times flummoxed by the subject he is grappling with, unable to understand reality in a society he expects is occupied by sane as well as devoted men and women. It is for this reason that Nyamnjoh's effort and approach in this rich, diverse, and equally delightful volume brings to mind W. H. Auden's idea of a topic being "only a peg on which to hang the poetry" as beyond theme as a whole, we see him experimenting with traditional poetic techniques taught in those colonized literary classes of yesterday.

With this volume, in any case, Nyamnjoh succeeds in modifying his literary portrait, but remains what he has always been before this venture: the conscience of African spaces in particular, and the world as a whole. That which looms large as his main concern, even as the poems celebrate, mourn, ridicule, lambast, and lament, is his fascination with the human being in society. It is with great pride then that I write this foreword for Nyamnjoh's latest achievement as, in an outstanding manner, it introduces to the public another side of him hitherto unknown to many— the poet.

Emmanuel Fru Doh
Century College Minnesota

Introduction

Just as ambidexterity strengthens a sportsperson and a good musician masters several instruments, a writer should be comfortable crossing over. Working in multiple genres reinforces writing overall. I have found that creative writing strengthens scholarly writing, and vice versa. Poetry reinforces prose and drama, and prose and drama feed poetry.

I am happy to share these poems that predate my short stories, play and novels. I wrote the poems as an outlet for my musings in the 1980s, mostly when I was in my early twenties. I did two years of high school at Cameroon College of Arts, Science and Technology (CCAST) in Bambili, 16 kilometres northeast of Bamenda, before studying for a bachelor's degree in sociology, philosophy and psychology at the University of Yaounde.

Rereading poems over 25 years after they were written is an interesting exercise. While I recognize myself in them and would rewrite them today, I also recognize that times and I have changed. Just as the world stays the same and changes, words reflect certain times and also ring true in others.

Let man be mostly moving as say the wise:
Twice never shall the same body and time be met.

The use of "man" in the poems refers to humankind, women and men, young and old, all peoples. I hope you find at least one poem in this collection that titillates or tantalizes... or more.

Francis B. Nyamnjoh
Cape Town
January 2011

1.

Learning and Leading

WHEN AROUND LIBRARIES

When around libraries books I see
Much with pleased joy I'm filled to know
Writings from time's beginnings
By those who stole neither sleep nor joy
For fear of not doing enough
For those who were and were to be

But these books that ate thought, work and time
Sleep in huge libraries unawakened
As decades drift away with more
While those for whom writers thought and think
Build better libraries for books to store
To better live, know and delight in dreams

TRIBUTE TO MADAM PHILOMINA NDONG BAWAK

I still see you silhouetted
Against the blackboards
Whitened with literary endeavours
Fresh from your reservoir of knowledge.

More and more as
The days draw by
That is what I see
And it makes me
Swim in a pool of gloom
To think you are no more.

How can I forget
Your last lesson on Chaucer
And the humour so befitting?
Even with a wild dunce mind,
How can I forget?

More and more as
The days draw by
That is what I recall
And it makes me
Swim in a pool of gloom
To think you are no more.

And the voice you used to teach was
An incarnation of heavenly harmony
Promoting the welfare of humankind.
Is it gone or singing still?

More and more as
The days draw by
The voice speaks
And it makes me
Swim in a pool of gloom
To think you are no more.

I still remember how in church
You smiled and shook hands with all.
The fold would wonder
If you were as learned as they heard.

More and more as
The days draw by,
That too I remember
And it makes me
Swim in a pool of gloom
To think you are no more.

Tell me where you went.
Were you received with exaltation?
Is your residence becoming?
If not, say, that we may appeal.

FLIGHT FROM SCIENCE

He left Biology,
Logic and Psychology.
He ran from Physics
And from Mathematics.
He befriended History
While enemy to Chemistry.
He took up Literature
And abandoned Architecture.
He went to Politics
Saying he was stranger to genetics.

But he was deceived;
The more I was avoided
The more my omnipresence
As the frightful Science.

He left school
Where I had a stool.
He went to his village
But there was a bridge
Which in a wink
Made him sink
The more in his fears.
He greeted me with a tear
And turned away
Taking a new way.

But wherever he went
He saw me in front
Ready to be his king
And ask him to sing.

He ran to the forest
Where he sat for a rest.
He looked around in disbelief
That he at last had found relief.
Hunger made him hunt for nuts
But deep in the forest were huts.

Makers of policies
And makers of wars
May not reject the truism
Though others take with cynicism
My eternal presence and relevance.

THE GENUINE INTELLECTUAL
to Dr. Bernard Fonlon, 1982
(four years before he died)

A happy couple of humble background gave him life.
In remotest Nso he passed infancy unnoticed noticing.
The mirror of culture sealed an image in his memory
And made Fonlon a child of the people, an object of
hope.

The whiteman saw in him a man, a bridge hard to damage.
He pictured mankind's harmonious co-existence with
daydream success.
He dreamt heaven gate-free with joyous expectancy
And made Fonlon a staff of his mission, an object of hope.

With relentless zeal he explored the whiteman's realm of
knowledge.
He drained the wells within and looked without to Nigeria.
Miraculously he traversed evil-infested rivers and forests,
And in Enugu in Fonlon: hope disappointed, hope
retained.

He forced the National University of Ireland to revise
her academic records.
He won a place of honour in the Classical Oxford of
England.
In France he enkindled a literary fire that flames at the
Sorbonne,
And Fonlon was: an investment by mankind, an object of
hope.

Back in Cameroon motherly arms unfolded in triumph.
The people recognised him and asked for a helping hand.
He headed many a ministry and administered justice,
And Fonlon was: the pride of the nation, an object of
hope.

He sowed the seeds of knowledge in the University of
Yaounde.
With cultural, religious, philosophical and political writings
he inspired creativity.

ABBIA – Cameroon Cultural Review – he founded and
directs,
And Fonlon is: a force to reckon with, an embodiment
of hope.

While he lives, he listens to the voices wailing in the
wilderness.
Let us seize and cage our double opportunity.
Let us read him and hear him and see him,
For Fonlon remains: A GENUINE INTELLECTUAL,
an object of hope.

TO THE LEADER

Sir, most dear,
Let people think;
Thought begets humanity.
Let feeling be free;
It's the gateway to truth.
Make not of ignorance a necklace;
By that you state your limits.

Avoid using the mirror;
It confirms your illusions.
Read on psychology
That mirrors your shams.
Be tolerant with critics;
That chases away droughts of mind,
For they alone your nose can see.

With the many be less sheepish;
It's sourced many a ruin.
Bathe in the waters of reconciliation;
It's a great form of hypnotism.
Let tact and intelligence sauce success,
Not fear imposed by caprice.
Wear for everyone a smile;
It humbles enemies better than missiles.

Let people in you an enigma see,
Not a noodle to be rolled and fingered.
Let your private life
Be the rest house of your public life.
With all this done,
The world won't have you to blame
When the baton on must pass.

A MADMAN

To those who called me mad
I thought them men so sad
Who can't learn
What in life to yearn.

I used to think so much
Of God and men of church
Who think and act
With neither course nor tact.

This made my aim in life
To create and stir much strife
Among men insistent
On God non-existent.

I thought and fought like mad
And made the fools so sad
With words that stabbed and harmed
And left their ears burnt and alarmed.

They then labelled me mad
And made my life so sad,
Burdened and fettered
As if unlettered.

What I did made me glad
But left all else sad
When they were made to bow
To my knowhow.

THE WORK OF A LEADER

You stood on Fako, that was twenty years and one ago.
I stood with you, banner in hand and ready to go.
You commanded, I obeyed.
You directed, I followed.

From Fako with force, to south to north to east, I flew.
In the storm the banner conquered all as it blew.
A life and death struggle;
A fight that lasted till '61.

But it ended in victory, with liberty in a cage.
You stood on Fako, this time to see the beast in a cage.

You stood on Fako, that was ten years and one ago.
I stood with you, pen in hand ready to sign at a go.
You directed, I moulded.
You commanded, I tended.

With encouraged patriotic enthusiasm, I vanished for days
seven.
North, south east and west went paper on pen.
Worthwhile work
Bore fruit in '72.
We had a nation created, realised our oneness.
You stood on Fako to beam with gladness.

You stand on Fako, you stand to share our harvest.
I stand with you, sling in hand – armed to guard the
harvest.
You motion, I impose.
You declare, I enforce.

WHEN THE JUJUS FELL LIKE ONE

Did you among those who
Saw the Jujus dance observe
With joy how they fell like one
In front of their hailed Fon?

Did you sense the brusque
Change of attitude in the people
When the Fon on their throne
Was indifferent to what fell like one?

Didn't it strike like lightening
How men like one may comport?
With no outside force came change
When the Fon belched pregnant indifference.

So did it strange you the next day
To find the throne unwarmed
And the kingmakers in shrines,
Praying to God for a Fon?

2.

Is Love an Illusion?

IS SHE FOR MEN?

Shall it be wrong if I call out, "Virgin Mary,
To the world I've been no more beautiful I've seen!"?
Tell me men, of a fairer fairy!
And naturalists, of a tree as green!

Glamorous mine, if all creatures could speak,
Your heels would their sonnets grace while you glide.
Can you recount divorce's start and peak?
You inspire men of infidelity to dream with pride.

Say who occupies your heart. If me, say!
But how can I while I'm not a god?
Which god can assure me safe stay
When this precious treasure I win? Which god!

Thousands may chase, to one is the beauty;
Some of grief will die, lonely is beauty.

LOVE TOKEN

Take this Dear:
A token of the inextinguishable love
I for you bear.
Think of its value in terms of love
Not money,
Which not a purpose serves
Other than a means of
Exchange of love tokens
To fuel Great Love.
It's from Martin,
Your Love Fountain.

A NEW YEAR ILLUSION

In the darkness of my room
A negative of posters
Projected the lady of my home
And placed her with immortals.

I saw her smile as I dreamt
Her walk the walls of my house,
With lovely hair long and kempt,
And apples beneath the blouse.

I turned sides and saw her stand
With hands outstretched to beckon
Me to walk, hand in hand,
And form with her a union.

I sprung out with hopes of love
Of the bed where I had seen
The lady calm as a dove,
With bright eyes, lovely and keen.

I onned the lights above
To see, to hear, smell and hold
This lady so full of love,
Of which I'd dreamt and told.

But all I saw on the walls
Wasn't the lady I'd dreamt,
Just posters on the walls,
Without hair so lovely and kempt.

My lady of love and home,
Whom I first saw in motion
On the walls of my cold room,
Was a New Year Illusion.

This good lady in the dark
First appeared on the first day
Of the new year like a spark –
Which I wished for long could stay.

What I want is love that stays;
Lady of my sweet dream,
I pray and wish union days
When I shall dish love in cream.

LOVE HUNGER

The first denied my love,
The second told me she never loves,
The third told me to come back in her twenties;
Were these milder ways of telling me off?

To the first I denied engagement;
To the second I knew I was wanting
For she had a fairer man in mind;
As for the third, I convinced her of her naivety.

Time passed, things changed.
The first, the second, the third,
With envious eyes, watched
Every move a fourth took to make me happy.

LOVELINE

Loveline saw couples there
Enacting under a tree
A language sweet to speak
By men who love to seek
In others the roots of life.

She stopped and used her eyes
To see them frozen like lice
Under the bonds of love,
Enacting words of love:
A language hardly known.

She watched the couples fall
By the tree green and tall.
She watched them act
And go along with no tact,
Keyed in unsanctioned love.

She saw the couples die
Under the tree so high,
Poisoned as they made love
By the hazards of love,
Which hang about the world.

If Loveline leads the world
Couples may better hold
The language sweet to speak
By those who love to seek
In others the roots of life.

A LOVEFUL MESSAGE

I met a man in
An old body, with a young mind
He was shallow mouthed and solidly worded
In a famished body, with a nourished soul
He was feeble limbed and powerfully veined
With disappearing eyes and sharpened ears

I must please his ears
For as he dies he shares
A loveful message:

Beware the story the eyes tell
The smiling snake has a harmful tail
Embrace he who least thinks of gain or loss
Consider the soul of life not the body of lust
Think twice of others' possibilities and impossibilities
Decide neither in hilarity nor stress
And the future becomes the fruition of today

3.

Sharp and Brusque

IN A WINK

Springs pass; the plant in luxury reigns;
Then in a wink, it vanishes as if it feigns.
Kinsmen may in ignorance Nature accuse –
Scarcely do they think of a burnt fuse!

DEPART NOT!

Depart not, Roof,
Forget not your duty.
Even Hell knows you father many,
Therefore depart not,
Forget not your dependants.
Even Satan could see and understand.
Oh! Oh! Do know!
Suicide God rejects!
Therefore stay rather and foot your bills.

SHARP AND BRUSQUE

A sudden wild disastrous drop
In her farm besides a lively crop
Which she had hoped to reap by dusk
Forced another to end, sharp and brusque

Father and I carried, sobbed and wept
Day and night where her corpse was kept
Till tear pools reflected our pale faces
And eyes swelled like upside-down ditches

Days went by as father thought deep
Why I failed to eat, drink and sleep
While I knew the dangers so great
Which he ceased not to enumerate

With mixed concern and sad pains
Created by vile death's brutal stains
Father went out to ease himself
And was asked to follow his wife

Wicked, rash and foolish death is
To leave alone in a big house
A little lone parentless child
With nothing to make life less wild

This I write to let the world know
That they may not care to ask how
A little girl so round
Vanished like a shallow wound

THE BABY

The baby slaughtered by
Coarse hands of inefficient youths
Via D & C of utmost danger
For eternity lost both face and name.

That baby that was murdered,
Who could say
What sex and number
It would have shown the world?

This baby that is gone
Would be justified in using a gun
To avenge its future ruined
And all it would have done.

Who can judge and how?
Whether of Good or Bad
Dust – what dust was it?
Dust that never came or went.

This baby you killed
Is now in death as free
As unfree it was when conceived
With sweet mutual skill.

TO PAY HER LOVER'S BILLS

To pay her lover's bills
Mother needed sleep pills,
A killer and two stones
And some spirits to toughen his bones.

To pay her lover's bills
Mother used rapid sleep pills
To soften father's bones
For a killer and two sharp stones.

Father thus sleep-pilled
Is netted and killed
By the killer with scaly stones
As he lies with weakened bones.

His corpse, round a stone imprisoned
In a way unsound and unreasoned,
Is with hope and prayer into Sanaga forced
To stay in water among rocks unremorsed.

To pay her lover's bills
Wicked mother with her skills
Demands a change of accounts
At CamBank of father's huge amounts.

But in doing what she did
Mother forgot about their kid
Who later in pain saw
What it meant to curse the law!

4.

Do Ordinary People Exist?

LIGHT

I passed in the park
Compounds sad and dark.
Men who smile day and night
Live a life without light
In these compounds sad and dark.

But, towering high and bright
Stands a lone house, mad with light.
Glowing hedges, grasses, and trees
Make a man live in peace
Here, towering high and, bright.

ALL ALONG

From childhood all along we've heard
Of such and such a great man gone
How they battled bravely and daringly
Making them named among the known
And kissed by Death at death.

From childhood all along we've lived
Looking round with pregnant hope
To read or hear of men that in the
Shadows lived and groped and hoped
But they lived not, nor ever died.

Only great men came and went
Ones that History tells us God sent
To cleanse, brighten and thrill the world
In which the small all along
May never be heard, nor live till death.

5.

Fathers and Sons

ONE IS ENOUGH

Now say it, Son:
Did you join hands with them, they,
The forces, harbingers of Evilways,
To slander your mother to ruin?

A hand against I dared not lift
And better so, as bent they were not an inch to shift.

Now say it, Son:
Of the foolish fiendish beastly guards
That duped by rusty coins played poorly their cards
And vanquish to us conveyed, were you one?

I lacked power to conjure honest words;
Vice and virtue interchanged
And better so, for I wanted not my mind exchanged.

Now say it, Son:
Are you of the insensible babbling lot
Who origin from apes, claim hot
And source, not to our Lord say, but the sun?

How could I no to science say, and to superstition yes?
And better so, for it's an idol in all our ways.

Now say it, Son:
If you knew evil not, would you shake hands?
Is a spark insufficient to set loose fire's fangs?
Are two bodies needed to make a great man?
You've failed in life your mission as a man!

SON

When at last you learn me gone,
Mourn me not, Dear.
But for sadistic men, you
Won't have sought to shed your tear.

Calm and screw your mind and swear
To think, to plan, to work a change
In those who, like a racing hare,
Are blind to cries of change.

Bag surprise when from your birth,
For long in vain awaited,
Mother alone lights your path
To spot where Death me awaited.

Shake your head and stir your grief;
Think of where best traps to place,
That your son may know no grief
In being born to see one face.

THE DILEMMA

PRESIDENT JOHN INQUISA:
I'm rattled with accorded pleasure
By your tamed lightning helter-skelter
That imprisons your hours of leisure
And chains you to my dubious matter.

Your response is pavlovian dog-like,
Unwarranted by the impudence
That stroke like an arbitrary pike
My summons highly absurdly tense.

My father has fingerprinted with
The treach'rous bait of the vain hearted;
Though morals draw me to this uncouth,
As pres'dent my debate is heated.

Between the nation's constitution
And my most filial committedness,
Render each your genuine opinion
That may tell us which horse to harness.

MR PAUL NEPOSA:
I brand all this a non matter
Unable to snatch away your sleep;
I see no problem in clear water
And wonder about the need for help.

Tell me between a man and his land
Who exercises the upper hand
When the man may be in need of sand
And has to look for it from the land?

Man's law is to serve man's very ends
To preserve fellow life God-given
Which he loves to see mult'pled in tens;
Law's man's bread baked in his own oven.

I don't crucify man's life for law,
A catalyst for his ambition,
And instead of man losing his war
I sell law to buy man and nation.

MR PETER PONEGA:
I'm not a slave to unfashioned love
That subjugates the devious minded
And destroys the seeds of reasoned love
Or junglises the block-headed.

Law's society's collective creation
To extinct man's animal drive,
Which flames in sporadic brute version,
And imbues him with zeal to see the state thrive.

Do your father what you would expect
From one to whom he isn't father
Or who has never learnt to respect
The treachery of a proud father.

I speak for the love of the many
And not the safety of a few,
Since roles pass from a hand to any,
But the many shall never be few.

The President dismissed them with thanks
And went behind his lovely house
Where with a rope and behind some tanks
He hooked his neck and died like a mouse.

6.

Outrage and Hope

CHRISTMAS

Christ was born in December
As I think I remember.
I was glad but I was poor
To go so near the door
Of a man born a leader
Though in a manger.

I saw him grow as a boy
Full of love and void of coy.
He would teach the wise in church
And be a crutch
To the miserable and weak
Whom he loved to cure and seek.

Then came a time he was slayed
In a garden as he prayed.
And leaving his disciples
Who loved to eat not apples
But the Holy Word of God,
He returned to his Lord God.

Men decided to observe
The birth of he who came to preserve
Man's fading face and unite
Firmly in God Black and White.
This was done in December
As I think I remember.

But I don't think December
Still means what I remember.
Christ has faded out of it
And it makes one feel so hit
How man may change for worst
When his finance is at best.

DESTINY

Is there some light in the world
Or does darkness reign everywhere?
Is there yet an honest being on earth
Or the germ has flown round the world?

Have children ever had fathers
Or is every situation like mine?
Are guardians always disappointing
Or is my case a peculiar one?

Does everyone on earth suffer
Or is suffering exclusively for me?
Is there another ardent believer in Fate
Or was I made to be his only discipline?

Let the world unfold itself:
Make me unique
Or make me a type;
Tell me I am lucky or unlucky.
Let the world speak!

NO MORE

He shouts screams and shoots
When bouts of dreams of lost roots
Revive wild emotions of childhood
Of blooming black brotherhood

The crowded cunning clowning court
That slavery showed his sailed kin at the port
Passed its judgement out of point, peace and place
And forced men to see his fierce faulty face

In waste he writes and reads of right
And hopes sweet days of sunshine bright
But in private is picked and pistoled
And the death-bringer boldly boasted freed

The pressed political public speaker
Fearing to leave his life as leader
Mounted a monument in honour
Of the man he vowed to greet no more

THE LONE CULPRIT

Has there once lived a man
Whom people so much loved to hate,
Who never passed by
Men of God without insult?

None so far is guilty
Safe the Devil
In whose life mischief, like
A tired shepherd, seeks refuge.

It's true the Devil
The lone culprit be
With frightening wings
Harmful only to good.

Shame oh! Shame then
On you, the only guilty
One is alone
With none but fools to comfort!

SALVATION
inspired the night a student died

A unique father we have, who had nor has a rival,
Safe the vile devil, to whom life is misery and pain,
Whose companions shall not see eternal life's arrival
For attempts to please the father are futile and in vain.

The devil dwells in them and earthly pleasures are their
will
But there is salvation and room enough in Heaven
That no one ever shall complain, "God had ill will."
Repent, repudiate sin, curse the devil, yourself leaven.

Purest, most kind, most loving, most merciful is He
Yet none is so thoughtful to hear His gospel.
Ruined by your sins, in perdition you float, weep for this.
The fire, the torments and laments to you mean a morsel.

Man hungry and thirsty, though the food be
If no efforts are made, shall of pain die.
Jesus is the love, the way to the merciful sea,
Believe in Him and you shall not die.

MASA*

Did you see it, brother; did you see the light?
Did you hear, sister; did you hear the messenger?
Did you agree, father; did you accept the philosophy?
Did you decide, mother; did you receive the preacher?

I saw the light, brother; I saw the spark from eternity.
It came to show the way, brother; it came through MASA.
I heard the messenger, sister; I heard the spear from ancestry.
It talked of cultural splendour; it agreed to break with conservatism.
It stated changing, father; it started through MASA.
I received the preacher, daughter; I received him from Freedomland.
He preached freedom; he preached freedom through MASA.

You were right, brother,
You were right, sister,
You were right, father,
You were right, mother.

With light,
With culture,
With change,
With freedom,
MASA would have succeeded!

---

* MASA: Mankon Students Association

YOU

Of all the woeful wars
History tells a tale
How soldiers died in vain
In fights *à contrecoeur*;
Did you know you were at fault?

Wilberforce's light
Shone into the dark minds
Of Black "beasts" oppressors
Generations gone;
Who than you sowed the source?

Africa's *cauchemar d'hier*
That's dulled her days,
Turned her role as slave
Into political pawn;
D'you ignore your part?

In what form will be
Our sorrow and supra-pains?
You seem our God on earth
Who plans and wills for man
But in whimful wickedness.

VOLATILE DREAMS

A warrior
With force and fuel of war
When things of state are staked
May use his words unweighed

A peasant
With a hoe and machete
To ease her task in life
May count on gifted friends

But the desert
That subdues aridity
With volatile dreams of hope
May from illusions die

7.

Ignorance and Freedom

REMARK!

Oh! Most prominent,
Most bright in the firmament
Of stars, Greatest,
Bless this hour, this day
When I become King.

Nature first unburdened me of
Ignorance   our greatest disease.
With joy unknown
I admitted your brilliance
Which sprinkles virtues
On a sea of unweeded minds
And remakes repentant devils
With a touch of utmost saintliness.

I received you free willed
And independent hearted.
And that: my difference with the fettered.

ENEMIES

They chased me with words,
Poisoned spears and swords;
At night their tree-hung rope
Sprinkled seeds of dead hope.

They targeted my shins
With death-bringing machines;
In phys'cal ag'ny
They sent me life's enemy –
A doctor so deathly.

They sent to school traps
Disguised as teachers
Who turned my heartiest friends
To begging stoogeful fiends
And passed me through gas-filled rooms –
Aggressive sciences' wombs.

What to them remained strange
Was lack of reach of range
When their forces were strong
Enough to mount the rung.

It struck the frosty hands
Of enmity in bands
To find present a prey
They could not waylay.

Never would they know
I was born to show
And teach men to be free
And stop fearing to be.

SOLUTIONS

When men drink and dance,
When children dream and fancy,
When women in trance
See in love the coins they fancy,
They are trying to solve in moonlight
What are problems in sunlight.

If in union you are with pretence
And think it a weakness
That with existence you should oneness share,
Won't you an ear lend with gladness
To those who know and use what's true,
Voicing on how to act and see and construe?

But suppose you don't since you won't
Want your pride and head down to put,
Would it hurt if the knowledged and wisdomed
Come you to class with the condemned
Who never did much to reject
Ignorance so abject?

8.

Power and Resistance

THE WHITEMEN OF GOD

They sailed night and day at sea
With angelic holiness and lambly dignity
They calmed the troubled waters with christly powers
Like the Eleventh Apollo they set foot on sinly Africa
The land of holy ventures, the land of endless battles

The welcoming poor gave them audience
In continuous distrust the noble remained
Their god germinated, their influence grew
And they succeeded over the divided African
The time was ripe, the battle was on

We rejected our cultures and ourselves
They broke down our families and destroyed our roots
Our gods vanished, our shrines disappeared
Anew we were born and like infants had to learn
We were taught to hear the bible of a god we knew by
proxy

They taught us to forgive and forget
They seized our land, children and women
They forced us to work in farms, mines and roads
They portioned us to clean and clear their yards
We were forced to forgive, forced to go to heaven

MUSIC THAT HARMS

What mosquito this is
Who threatens friends of his
And makes them lose their rest
With music made from west!

Music music always
Music from west with ways
Of dance and sing and do
And ways of thinking too.

Music in time and place
Respect my right of space
That to me makes a man
Not noise from music can.

Let me test our friendship
And ask him bring by ship
Bundles of nets wide like mats
To trap music that harms like rats.

He laughed and termed me mad
And said he couldn't be sad
Keeping me in life
Anguishing in strife.

For a fight he calls me,
Of means and skill and sense,
If I ignore my kin.

A COMPLEX SITUATION

Did we invite them, like does friend a friend?
Could we fall in love with a civilisation vile and wild?
Did we shake hands with exploitation and deception?
Did we yearn for schools, crime and corruption?
Could we share a house with domination cold and
murderous?

Was it not at birth we started life with thought?
Could we live a culture borrowed or brought?
Was it not long ago we lived in societies well and fine?
Did not our parents bring us up to rise and shine?
Did we ever acknowledge poverty in our ways?

Why then accept a position of abject rejection?
Why be submerged by waves of vilelish domination?
Why be fettered away by lies and pretentious saintliness?
Why pass for superior-inferiors with slave-like readiness?
Why wear their cap of absolute foolishness?

THE RUMOUR WENT

The rumour comes roaring in the storm
And withdraws like a weakened sea wave,
To come again with newly born effort.
In the west, north, south and east they say,
The Electron Sorcerer solves all.

With problems yearning quick solutions,
I have come to determine your myth.
Scan my basket filled with black problems
And answer rightly within a wink.

"Consultation without payment,
Answer to question negative.
Price asked; information board reads:
Cocoa, gold, decision right lost.
Quick – accurated quick action."

Years tens ago peace died of heat
When his black feather bag was spoilt
And his sparkled smile mud-buried
By men who claimed you made them live.
Could you bring us back our Dear Peace?

"Consultation abstract; figureless
Answer to question negative.
Price to pay however; news board reads:
Oil, timber, simpleton in politics.
Quick – accurated quick action."

Electron Sorcerer solves all,
The rumour went from mouth to ear.
Yes, he solves really every purse;
Payment for service not rendered.

MY GRIEVOUS BED
written at the request of Aban

Why all these torments by thy hands
That I thy cruelty for half a day endure,
Consuming thy never ceasing demands?
Great are my laments and heavy the fortune.
Such feeble-minded creatures as you
Ought no shame evade!

Thy vile coins me did from my master purchase.
Though thine, a sheep I'm not!
Tell me then how I deserve all this!
An individual I am in action and thought.
Domination should not be
For you lack the guarantee.

God himself the accounts shall record
And these accounts shall these include:
My misuse without accord,
Thy lack of a strong moral code,
My never failing satisfaction
With thy destructive inclination.

HE DIED IN PEACE ON DECK

He muttered harsh words of hope
To God as with his thick rope
He tied a slave to oppression
And reaped from forced submission.

He lived heathen seclusion
And prayed God for oblivion
Of the less qualified race,
Blest with a repulsive face.

As a matter of principle
He told every disciple
To pray to God he loved
Before theft of what he craved.

He killed his rivals with tact,
Allied with vice in a pact
And dedicated all wars
To the God of his just cause.

He conquered giant churches
But never went on crutches
Nor ever suffered headache
Till he died in peace on deck.

RESOLUTIONS

It's been resolved with unanimity
Times before, by nations so capable;
Many a painful year has come and come
With countless moments of silence for men
Whom state histories have judged more action full.

It's been resolved with unanimity
By world bodies capable of great flames;
It's been resolved to denounce with words,
Words harsh enough for those who can hear
But senseless, harmless words to the earless.

It's been resolved with unanimity
When much blood has poured for lost liberty;
Words radioed to revive lives ruined by guns
Have been intended for fashioned deafness,
Favourable to words smeared with harshness.

It's been resolved with unanimity
By great nations blessed by history and fate
To kill with mere words those who kill with guns
And fetter in threes young black seekers of freedom
Who ignored the illusions of words of wisdom.

Francis B. Nyamnjoh

AMOK!
about the 1983 projection of the film Amok at Capitol Cinema in Yaounde

Perfect reflection of southern African Black realities,
Humans exposed to inhuman tortures,
Pains great in body and soul,
Mass molestation and extermination.
Blacks contest the Idea of a greater Hell.

BUT IN THEM ALL

Neither in colour,
Nor in colonisation
And domination,
Nor in deception
And exploitation,
Nor in molestation
And extermination
Lies the solution
To universal problems,
But in them all lies their origin.

YET

They send me sorrow-smeared words
Asking firmly for a redress with swords
And promising their voice and hand
Till they all lie below the sand.

Yet I think among them all
In gowns are men, slim, dark and tall,
Who pace the darkest corners in town
With hopeful chaplets to see me down.

ERUPTIONS

Our mountain's for long been silent,
Silent from birth, they say.
It's kept its calm in the storms,
Storms active the world over.

I think it's time for noise,
Time for graves to erupt,
Time for them to spit out
The hungry lions that for long have slept.

It's true the angered lions for long have slept
But it isn't true they will cease to sleep
For of late an abler lion hunter surfaced
And taught them to hunger and anger with smile.

I think it waited overly much
Its hungry lions up to wake,
Thought of it quite too late
Only to find them roar like paper lions.

REASSURANCE

When the earth hardens as the sun burns,
Man feels reassured when he turns
To the sight of a little palm
Cured with a baobab balm.

But if space enoughs many lives
Bees should strive for more hives
To defuse the danger of struggle
Over a giggle-dulling trifle.

Only hardwork alone can open the door
To motive-ridden Aid To The Poor
Without fear of guilt or debasement
Nor of disenchanted devoicement.

9.

Peacemakers

MY DUTY

To the state I dedicate
To live a life soft and sound and deep
Which my compatriots may emulate
Which like game hunters may catch and keep
As mirror for citizens to come.

I pledge our state's ideals to uphold
Which best of reasons makes me embrace
As superb for all young and old
To join the mask and conceal my face
Not to dance out of oneness of tune.

My role: keep the rules I vow,
Never this to say and mean but that,
Never food and drink to take anyhow,
Never the fence to sit like a cat
But duty do and let duty be done.

DREGS OF WAR

When all our wars are fought
And all our soldiers killed
Let's release our frozen thought
And turn to those we've chilled.

Those whose thoughts and actions
Are full of salt for man.
Face war's wicked sanctions,
War void of aim and plan.

These dregs of war may pass
From door to door with hats
Or wait at end of mass
Or steal with skill or rats.

They may meet dubious rich
And sign papers of faith
After every empty speech
To search for life a path.

Thus war may make of man
A nameless faceless tool
A voiceless choiceless fan
For those with choice to fool.

MAKERS OF PEACE

Pride is ours as makers of peace
When men of East are more at ease.
So let's all ally our arms
And fight against makers of wars.

Ours would be a war of peace
And men that die would die for peace.
We should all fight and fight like men
And chase the lions out of their den.

We all know their dangers so great
Who in war or peace rest a threat.
Let's fight then in peace or in wars
And subdue these makers of wars.

Because it's a fight of East and West
A midway battleground is best
Which if destroyed during the wars
Is a sacrifice for great peace.

QUELQUE CHOSE

Je voulais vous dire quelque chose,
Quelque chose d'important, de bon,
De bon comme un arbre à plusieurs branches,
Comme une hydre à plusieurs bras.

Oui, je voulais vous dire cette chose,
Et je compte sur vous, je compte sur tous,
Comme l'arbre compte sur ses branches,
Comme l'hydre compte sur ses bras.

Je compte sur vous, je compte sur tous
Pour faire mes guerres, pour vaincre les ennemies,
Pour construire le pays, pour faire le progrès,
Pour lutter contre les vices et chercher les vertus.

J'ai dit ce que je voulais vous dire:
Que la vie se vit comme une tête des têtes,
Que l'action est toujours l'unité d'actions
Et que la nation est parfaite selon notre voix.

10.

Certain and Uncertain

WHAT THE WISE SAY

Yesterday he made me think him friendly;
Unfriendly today he is unlike yesterday.
Change tomorrow for the former;
Later to be revisited isn't strange.

And year last he said we never shall again
Strain in give-and-take and shake of hand;
Let man be mostly moving as say the wise:
Twice never shall the same body and time be met.

Wise and poor, rich and foolish alike
Strike in life but the wicked chord of vice
To reward or revenge out of time and turn,
If we take as truth what the wise say.

SHOW ME TO BAMENDA

It's Bamenda I'm in search of.

That I think you cannot reach.

What you mean I know not
But I think I'm quite hot
About going there by air.

You may as well eat your hair
For I'm blind to queer dreams
Strange to our realms.

I may go by way of sea.

She has never seen the sea.

Show me the way by car.

There was a way to her
Which strangely is no longer.

Does it mean I must hunger?
What if I go by train?

You may begin to strain
But you may reach it by foot
If Bamenda must be got.

If that's the way I cannot!
It's Bamenda I'm in search of!

That I think you cannot reach!

ALL HAVE CHANGED

The people I left
The things I left
The place I left.
All have changed, yet remain intact.
I knew a phase; now I see another.

Nature was green, fresh and lively; that I knew.

In union are a past, a present and a crisis.
Innocent children – mushrooms in precipitation.
The ultimate destroyer rests assured.
The real change is obvious;
The rest is seeming.
Yet I am deceived;
Someone somewhere in triumph smiles.

The place I left
The things I left
The people I left.
Know well enough,
It's I that's changed.

I'M CERTAIN

If only I this midnight
Heavy slumber's batt'ring wings
Can aside with all my might
Try my pregnant best to push
And shun their calls sweet to take,
To everybody at dawn
I'm certain to take a cake.

THE AMBIGUITY OF HAZARDS

Hazards without Masters
Masters foolish Masters
That confide sheepishly
In dangers so deathly
To master weaker hazards